My Generations

A Course in Jewish Family History

ARTHUR KURZWEIL

BEHRMAN HOUSE

ACKNOWLEDGMENTS

I am grateful to many friends, teachers, colleagues and organizations for their help with this book. Especially: Dr. Harold Wise, Danny Siegel, Rabbi Malcolm Stern, Steven W. Siegel, Jacob Behrman, Adam Bengal, Seymour Rossel, Dr. Lucjan Dobroszycki, Julian Bach, The Coalition for Alternatives in Jewish Education, Sesil Lissberger, Dr. Alan Kay, the JWB Lecture Bureau, the Kurzweil Family Circle, the New York Public Library—Jewish Division, the YIVO Institute for Jewish Research and Elie Wiesel. Thank you for helping the search for my Jewish family history to become a personal pilgrimage and a tool for learning.

I wish to also thank my family members around the world who have encouraged and helped me. In particular: Michele Zoltan, Maurice Gottlieb, Sam Kurzweil, Rose Kurzweil, Zsuzsa Barta, Hilda Kurzweil, Joseph Schlaf, and Ken Kurzweil. A special word of thanks and love are due my parents, Saul and Evelyn Kurzweil, for the spark of Torah they passed from their parents to me.

Although many people assisted with this book, it is my editor and friend, Ruby Strauss, to whom my deepest thanks go.

A.K.

The Cover: Superimposed on this 18th century Italian *ketubah* (Jewish marriage document) are Eli and Dobroh Kurzweil and their children. The photograph was taken in Dobromil, Poland. On July 29, 1942 they were taken, along with many other of the author's relatives, to a Nazi death camp. They were murdered. May their memory be for a blessing.

COVER / BOOK DESIGN BY ABNER GRABOFF

© COPYRIGHT 1983 BY ARTHUR KURZWEIL

PUBLISHED BY BEHRMAN HOUSE, INC.
Springfield, New Jersey 07081
www.behrmanhouse.com
ISBN: 978-0-87441-383-0

MANUFACTURED IN THE UNITED STATES OF AMERICA

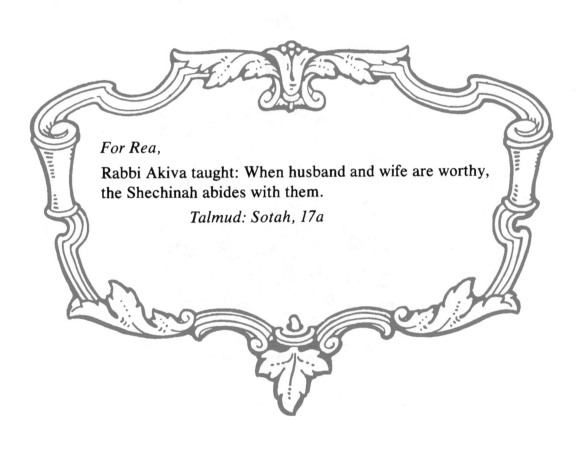

For Rea,

Rabbi Akiva taught: When husband and wife are worthy, the Shechinah abides with them.

Talmud: Sotah, 17a

WHEN
I GIVE
I GIVE
MYSELF

This Book Belongs To:

Contents

YOU ARE HERE

CHAPTER 1

WHERE ARE YOU?

Where are you—right now? Are you sitting in a classroom? Are you at home in your room? Are you on a bus? In a car? Sitting at the kitchen table? There are over 4 billion (4,000,000,000) people in the world and each of us is somewhere.

Snap your fingers right this second. You are making a sound at the most recent moment in all of history. Of course, as soon as the "snap" is over, another moment of history has passed, and then another, and so on. With each moment, history continues. It is interesting to think that while today is today, tomorrow today will be yesterday. And two days from now, tomorrow will become yesterday!

Another way to put it is this: cars ride on roads, boats ride on water, and history rides on "time." Just like a car or a boat, history travels along going from one moment to the next.

You have been traveling—in history—until this very moment. Each day goes by and with each passing day, you do more things, go more places, and think more thoughts. You are moving along—with history. And for some reason, right at this moment, you have ended up exactly where you are!

One of the realities of history is that people travel from place to place, making new homes for themselves along the way. People have been leaving home and making new homes elsewhere since the beginning of time. In fact, one could say that history is, in part, the story of people and families moving from one place to another. At one point, your parents married and established a home together. Then, you were born and joined their migration.

Almost every person living in the United States is an immigrant, or a descendant of immigrants. Most Jewish families in America have not been here very long at all. In fact, it probably was either your grandparents or your great grandparents who were the immigrants in your family. Of course, this does not apply to everyone. You may be an immigrant yourself. It is also possible that your family was in America long before your great grandparents were born. Some Jewish families have been in America for a few hundred years.

In this book, you will explore your Jewish connections. You will examine the lives of your ancestors to understand the choices they faced and the decisions they made. Learning about what came before will help you understand your own personal history.

You will have the opportunity, in this book, to record your own family history. And some day, be it a month, a year, or a century from now, someone in your family will look at this book and learn all about you.

MY FATHER CAME TO AMERICA WHEN HE WAS EIGHT YEARS old. He never returned to his hometown, Dobromil, in Eastern Europe. Yet he remembers almost every detail of the neighborhood where he lived. I found a street map of my father's town in a rare library book. When I showed it to him, he was able to remember and point out many of the places where his friends had lived and things had happened in his childhood. My father was almost able to draw a map of his hometown by himself.

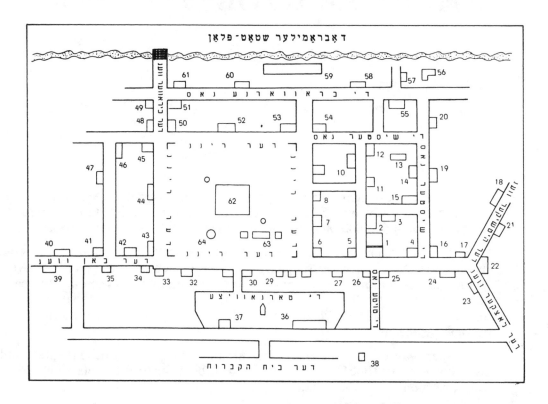

Dobromil.

My Neighborhood

In the space below, draw a map of your neighborhood. Make it as detailed as you can. Try to include your house, synagogue, library, school and the homes of close friends. If you could ask your great-great grandfather to draw a map of his neighborhood what elements would you be interested in seeing? The answer to this question might give you some additional things to include in your map for the future generations of your family.

WHEN I DECIDED TO TRAVEL TO THE TOWNS IN EASTERN EUROPE once called ''home'' by my family, I didn't know what to expect. But something drew me to those places, something powerful that I cannot fully explain. In a small rented car, I drove from town to town, searching for some remnant of my family's past.

When I arrived in Przemysl, the place of my great-grandfather's birth over 115 years ago, I felt as though I had been there before. I had never visited that town, yet somehow it all seemed familiar—the streets, the shops, the market, the Jewish cemetery. Exploring Przemysl, I located some of the houses where my family had lived before the Holocaust. In a tiny, rural town in northeast Hungary, I stood before the grave of my great-great grandmother. I walked the streets that were known by my ancestors for generations.

One day, while driving through the backroads of the part of Poland once known as Galicia, I realized that I had made a wrong turn. Rather than turning back, I decided to see where my ''error'' would lead me. I came to a road sign with the word BELZEC on it. I had heard about Belzec. For in that Polish town, thousands of Jews—including many members of the Kurzweil family—had been murdered in the Nazi Death Camp that stood on that spot. Today, there is nothing. Nothing but a sign and a memory.

This building in Przemysl, Poland is now a bus garage. It was once a synagogue.

A quiet road in Kantorjanosi, Hungary, birthplace of my great-great-grandfather, Tvi Hersh Klein.

Branches of the Kurzweil family lived on this street in Przemysl, Poland.

Nyirbator, Hungary was the birthplace of my grandmother, Helen Klein.

Members of the Kurzweil family lived in these two houses in Jaraslaw, Poland before the Holocaust.

My Community

There are many places to mount photographs in this book. A family historian appreciates the value of photographs and never pastes an original photograph in a book. So unless you have a copy of a photo or its negative in a safe place, do not paste it here. Fortunately, most photocopy machines can reproduce photographs and these reproductions are perfect to mount on this page and the others like it. (Your photos need not fit inside the photographic corner mounts.)

MY HOME   MY SYNAGOGUE

MY SCHOOL

Family Residence Record MY RELATIVES IN THE UNITED STATES

These pages of names, addresses and telephone numbers can become a central directory for all the members of your family. Don't worry about putting the list in alphabetical order. Just fill in the necessary information. Addresses change from time to time so use a pencil, not a pen. Begin by asking your parents for addresses and phone numbers of relatives. Then call close relatives and ask them for similar information. If you select the right people to ask, your FAMILY RESIDENCE RECORD can become the most complete list of your relatives anywhere.

NAME _____

ADDRESS _____

_____

TELEPHONE NUMBER _____

NAME _____

ADDRESS _____

_____

TELEPHONE NUMBER _____

NAME _____

ADDRESS _____

_____

TELEPHONE NUMBER _____

NAME _____

ADDRESS _____

_____

TELEPHONE NUMBER _____

NAME _____

ADDRESS _____

_____

TELEPHONE NUMBER _____

NAME _____

ADDRESS _____

_____

TELEPHONE NUMBER _____

NAME _____

ADDRESS _____

_____

TELEPHONE NUMBER _____

NAME _____

ADDRESS _____

_____

TELEPHONE NUMBER _____

NAME _____

ADDRESS _____

_____

TELEPHONE NUMBER _____

NAME _____

ADDRESS _____

_____

TELEPHONE NUMBER _____

NAME _____

ADDRESS _____

_____

TELEPHONE NUMBER _____

NAME _____

ADDRESS _____

_____

TELEPHONE NUMBER _____

NAME _____

ADDRESS _____

_____

TELEPHONE NUMBER _____

NAME _____

ADDRESS _____

_____

TELEPHONE NUMBER _____

NAME _____

ADDRESS _____

_____

TELEPHONE NUMBER _____

NAME _____

ADDRESS _____

_____

TELEPHONE NUMBER _____

NAME _____

ADDRESS _____

_____

TELEPHONE NUMBER _____

NAME _____

ADDRESS _____

_____

TELEPHONE NUMBER _____

NAME _____

ADDRESS _____

_____

TELEPHONE NUMBER _____

NAME _____

ADDRESS _____

_____

TELEPHONE NUMBER _____

NAME _____

ADDRESS _____

_____

TELEPHONE NUMBER _____

NAME _____

ADDRESS _____

_____

TELEPHONE NUMBER _____

Family Residence Record MY RELATIVES IN OTHER COUNTRIES

Do you have family living outside of the United States? Perhaps you have relatives in Canada or in South America, in Europe or in Israel. These names, addresses and phone numbers are often the most difficult to obtain, but there are probably people in your family who have this information. Find them and record this important data.

NAME _____

ADDRESS _____

_____

TELEPHONE NUMBER _____

NAME _____

ADDRESS _____

_____

TELEPHONE NUMBER _____

NAME _____

ADDRESS _____

_____

TELEPHONE NUMBER _____

NAME _____

ADDRESS _____

_____

TELEPHONE NUMBER _____

NAME _____

ADDRESS _____

_____

TELEPHONE NUMBER _____

NAME _____

ADDRESS _____

_____

TELEPHONE NUMBER _____

NAME _____

ADDRESS _____

_____

TELEPHONE NUMBER _____

NAME _____

ADDRESS _____

_____

TELEPHONE NUMBER _____

NAME _____

ADDRESS _____

_____

TELEPHONE NUMBER _____

NAME _____

ADDRESS _____

_____

TELEPHONE NUMBER _____

WHERE I HAVE LIVED

Your move—from your last home to your present home—is a part of the history of Jewish migration. In the same way that we write about Jews in the 1600's by saying, "Where did Jews live in those days?", so, too, will people one hundred years from now ask about the Jews of today. *Your* story will become a part of Jewish history!

ADDRESS _____

_____

DATES _____

ADDRESS _____

_____

DATES _____

ADDRESS _____

_____

DATES _____

ADDRESS _____

_____

DATES _____

ADDRESS _____

_____

DATES _____

ADDRESS _____

_____

DATES _____

BETWEEN THE YEARS 1880 AND 1925, NEARLY 2½ MILLION JEWS
came to America. They traveled by steamship. The journey took from seven to
ten days. Conditions on board were cramped and difficult. The fare of $35.00
was an enormous expense for the average Jew in those days.

LIST OR MANIFEST OF ALIEN PASSENGERS FOR THE UNITED

S.S. AQUITANIA   Passengers sailing from SOUTHAMPTON   18TH MAY, 19 29.

No. on List	HEAD-TAX STATUS	Family name	Given name	Age Yrs.	Mos.	Sex	Married or single	Calling or occupation	Able to Read	Nationality (Country of which citizen or subject)	Race or people	Place of birth Country	City or town	Immigration Visa Number	Issued at	Date	Last permanent residence Country	City or town
17		KURZWEIL	MANIA	34		F	M	HSWIFE	YES	JEWISH	YES POLAND	HEBREW	POLAND	DOBROMIL	3827	Warsaw	2.4.29	POLAND	DOBROMIL
18	UNDER 16	KURZWEIL	RAFAL	9		M	S	STUDENT	YES	JEWISH	YES POLAND	HEBREW	POLAND	DOBROMIL	3828	Warsaw	2.4.29	POLAND	DOBROMIL
19	UNDER 16	KURZWEIL	SZAUL	7		M	S	CHILD	NO	child	NO POLAND	HEBREW	POLAND	DOBROMIL	3829	Warsaw	2.4.29	POLAND	DOBROMIL
20	UNDER 16	KURZWEIL	RUCHLA	5		F	S	CHILD	NO	child	NO POLAND	HEBREW	POLAND	DOBROMIL	3830	Warsaw	2.4.29	POLAND	DOBROMIL

MOST IMMIGRANTS CAME TO AMERICA BY STEAMSHIP. I OFTEN imagine what it must have been like to leave home and sail across the rough and dangerous waters of the Atlantic Ocean.

The captain of the ship kept a list of his passengers, officially known as the ship's manifest. He gave it to the immigration officials at the port of entry. The list included the name of each passenger, age, occupation, and town and country of origin.

I obtained my father's passenger list from the National Archives in Washington, D.C. The list helps me to imagine a chapter in *my* history. The mass migration of Jews to America has been written about in dozens of books—but no book has sparked my imagination as much as the actual manifest of the ship which brought a piece of *me* to America.

My Immigrant Ancestors

The people in your family who came from another country to live in the United States are your "immigrant ancestors." Perhaps you yourself are an immigrant. Who were the individuals in your family who made the decision to leave their homes and travel to America? Not only is this information interesting in itself (their decisions certainly had great impact on your life) but it will help you when you do further research.

NAME   RELATIONSHIP TO ME

EMIGRATED FROM   NAME OF SHIP   PORT OF ENTRY

DATE OF ARRIVAL   AGE UPON ARRIVAL   PLACE OF SETTLEMENT

OTHER PEOPLE WHO SHARED THE JOURNEY

NAME   RELATIONSHIP TO ME

EMIGRATED FROM   NAME OF SHIP   PORT OF ENTRY

DATE OF ARRIVAL   AGE UPON ARRIVAL   PLACE OF SETTLEMENT

OTHER PEOPLE WHO SHARED THE JOURNEY

NAME   RELATIONSHIP TO ME

EMIGRATED FROM   NAME OF SHIP   PORT OF ENTRY

DATE OF ARRIVAL   AGE UPON ARRIVAL   PLACE OF SETTLEMENT

OTHER PEOPLE WHO SHARED THE JOURNEY

NAME _____ RELATIONSHIP TO ME _____

EMIGRATED FROM _____ NAME OF SHIP _____ PORT OF ENTRY _____

DATE OF ARRIVAL _____ AGE UPON ARRIVAL _____ PLACE OF SETTLEMENT _____

OTHER PEOPLE WHO SHARED THE JOURNEY _____

NAME _____ RELATIONSHIP TO ME _____

EMIGRATED FROM _____ NAME OF SHIP _____ PORT OF ENTRY _____

DATE OF ARRIVAL _____ AGE UPON ARRIVAL _____ PLACE OF SETTLEMENT _____

OTHER PEOPLE WHO SHARED THE JOURNEY _____

NAME _____ RELATIONSHIP TO ME _____

EMIGRATED FROM _____ NAME OF SHIP _____ PORT OF ENTRY _____

DATE OF ARRIVAL _____ AGE UPON ARRIVAL _____ PLACE OF SETTLEMENT _____

OTHER PEOPLE WHO SHARED THE JOURNEY _____

MY GRANDMOTHER, MOLLIE ENNIS KURZWEIL, POSED FOR the picture above with her three children. Her husband, my grandfather, is not in the picture. The photograph was taken in Poland and he was already working in America. It took him five years to earn the money necessary to bring his wife and children to America. The picture below, of the same three children, was taken fifty years later in the United States.

On August 27, 1923, my grandfather, Julius Kurzweil, boarded the steamship Tyrrhenia. He was leaving Europe—his family's home for generations. Ten days later, on September 6, the ship arrived in New York. This is my grandfather's passport photo.

In January, 1908, when my grandmother Helen Klein was just a teenager, she boarded the steamship Vaderland. Leaving her home, her friends and most of her family, she came to settle in the United States.

On January 14, 1907, my grandfather Samuel L. Gottlieb boarded the steamship Cronprinzes Cecilie. Traveling alone to America, he surely could not have imagined that the family he left behind would be murdered during the Holocaust.

Photographs of My Immigrant Ancestors

Mount copies of photographs or photocopies here—not the originals.

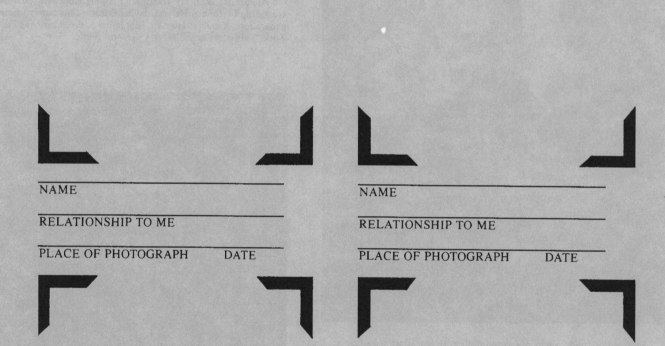

NAME _____

RELATIONSHIP TO ME _____

PLACE OF PHOTOGRAPH _____ DATE _____

NAME _____

RELATIONSHIP TO ME _____

PLACE OF PHOTOGRAPH _____ DATE _____

NAME _____

RELATIONSHIP TO ME _____

PLACE OF PHOTOGRAPH _____ DATE _____

NAME _____

RELATIONSHIP TO ME _____

PLACE OF PHOTOGRAPH _____ DATE _____

NAME _____

RELATIONSHIP TO ME _____

PLACE OF PHOTOGRAPH   DATE

NAME _____

RELATIONSHIP TO ME _____

PLACE OF PHOTOGRAPH   DATE

NAME _____

RELATIONSHIP TO ME _____

PLACE OF PHOTOGRAPH   DATE

NAME _____

RELATIONSHIP TO ME _____

PLACE OF PHOTOGRAPH   DATE

CHAPTER 2

WHERE DID YOU COME FROM?

My brother teaches biology; I teach Jewish history and genealogy. We often get into lengthy discussions and we are often on opposite sides of the argument. But there is one thing that both my brother and I agree on with ease: all of our ancestors are in each of us.

My brother looks at a person from a biologist's point of view and sees a wide variety of physical characteristics: color of hair, color of eyes, shape of face, and with the aid of laboratory equipment he sees the structure of cells as well. In each case, my brother not only sees the people he examines but also their parents. The color of your eyes, for example, is determined by the color of your parents' eyes. But actually, that's not exactly true—because we also have to look at your grandparents' eyes—which, as you know, were determined by *their* parents' eyes, and so forth.

You look the way you look in large part because your ancestors looked the way they looked. When you look in the mirror and see the color of your eyes, you are seeing the latest combination of what the generations before you produced. It is not inaccurate to say that you are literally made of your *thousands* of ancestors.

Of course, once I hear the word "ancestors" my ears perk up since, as I said, one of my interests is genealogy. And I am startled to hear my brother talk about ancestors since *I'm* the genealogist in the family; he's the biologist. And this is where we meet in full agreement.

Where do our "thousands" of ancestors come from? Do we really have that many? A little simple arithmetic will answer that question. Think about your ancestors for a moment; your two parents, four grandparents, eight great-grandparents, and so on. Can you see how this would add up to a lot of people?

If you were adopted, or if you have more than two parents due to divorce or death, you are probably thinking about this. The truth is that there are many people whose family history is not so simple as to allow them to think about two parents, four grandparents, and so on. Most families do not have such simple, neat histories. In fact, as a genealogist who has traced the families of many, many people, I would safely say that *no* family in the world would be able to do simple arithmetic to add up all their ancestors.

Every family is different. No two families are alike. Every family history is different. Keep this in mind as you record your family history. Adapt this book to your own family. Use the book as a tool, keeping in mind that you and your family are unique!

This is a facsimile of a birth certificate. If you cannot locate your own, fill in the spaces to record the information usually found on birth certificates. If you have your actual birth certificate, photocopy it and paste it over the one provided.

Birth Registration Certificate

CITY OF _____ COUNTY OF _____

_____

NAME   SEX   PLACE OF BIRTH

_____

DATE OF BIRTH   DAY OF WEEK   TIME OF BIRTH

_____

FATHER'S NAME   AGE   BIRTHPLACE

_____

MOTHER'S NAME   AGE   BIRTHPLACE

_____

DOCTOR

_____

STATE OF

One of the most ancient and sacred duties in Jewish tradition is the Brit Milah. On the eighth day of life, a Jewish boy is circumcised according to Jewish custom and ritual. If you can locate your Brit Milah Certificate, photocopy it and paste it over the one provided. If not, complete the one provided to record this important event in your Jewish life.

Brit Milah Certificate

In conformity with the hallowed observance of the Jewish faith

_____

son of _____

and _____

was brought into the covenant of Abraham and given the Hebrew name of

_____

at _____

DATE OF BIRTH   19 _____

57 _____

It is Jewish custom to name baby girls and boys at an official ceremony. Perhaps you can locate the certificate of your naming. If so, paste a copy here. If not, complete this certificate with the necessary information.

CERTIFICATE FOR
NAMING A CHILD

IN CONFORMITY
WITH JEWISH TRADITION

_____

CHILD OF

_____

WAS NAMED AND BLESSED IN THE SANCTUARY OF THE LORD

_____

CONGREGATION

_____

CITY

_____

AND GIVEN THE HEBREW NAME OF

_____

MAY IT BECOME A NAME HONORED IN THE HOUSEHOLD OF ISRAEL

DATE OF NAMING

_____ 19 __   _____ 57 __

My Father's Genealogy

MY GRANDFATHER
(MY FATHER'S FATHER)

NAME _____

BORN _____
      DATE   PLACE

MARRIED _____
           DATE   PLACE

DIED _____
      DATE   PLACE

MY FATHER

NAME _____

BORN _____
      DATE   PLACE

MARRIED _____
            DATE   PLACE

DIED _____
      DATE   PLACE

MY GRANDMOTHER
(MY FATHER'S MOTHER)

NAME _____

BORN _____
      DATE   PLACE

MARRIED _____
            DATE   PLACE

DIED _____
      DATE   PLACE

MY GREAT GRANDFATHER
(MY FATHER'S FATHER'S FATHER)

NAME _____

BORN _____
      DATE   PLACE

MARRIED _____
         DATE   PLACE

DIED _____
      DATE   PLACE

MY GREAT GRANDMOTHER
(MY FATHER'S FATHER'S MOTHER)

NAME _____

BORN _____
      DATE   PLACE

MARRIED _____
         DATE   PLACE

DIED _____
      DATE   PLACE

MY GREAT GRANDFATHER
(MY FATHER'S MOTHER'S FATHER)

NAME _____

BORN _____
      DATE   PLACE

MARRIED _____
         DATE   PLACE

DIED _____
      DATE   PLACE

MY GREAT GRANDMOTHER
(MY FATHER'S MOTHER'S MOTHER)

NAME _____

BORN _____
      DATE   PLACE

MARRIED _____
         DATE   PLACE

DIED _____
      DATE   PLACE

MY GRANDFATHER
(MY MOTHER'S FATHER)

NAME _____

BORN _____
        DATE   PLACE

MARRIED _____
        DATE   PLACE

DIED _____
        DATE   PLACE

MY MOTHER

NAME _____

BORN _____
        DATE   PLACE

MARRIED _____
        DATE   PLACE

DIED _____
        DATE   PLACE

MY GRANDMOTHER
(MY MOTHER'S MOTHER)

NAME _____

BORN _____
        DATE   PLACE

MARRIED _____
        DATE   PLACE

DIED _____
        DATE   PLACE

MY GREAT GRANDFATHER
(MY MOTHER'S FATHER'S FATHER)

NAME _____

BORN _____
DATE   PLACE

MARRIED _____
DATE   PLACE

DIED _____
DATE   PLACE

MY GREAT GRANDMOTHER
(MY MOTHER'S FATHER'S MOTHER)

NAME _____

BORN _____
DATE   PLACE

MARRIED _____
DATE   PLACE

DIED _____
DATE   PLACE

MY GREAT GRANDFATHER
(MY MOTHER'S MOTHER'S FATHER)

NAME _____

BORN _____
DATE   PLACE

MARRIED _____
DATE   PLACE

DIED _____
DATE   PLACE

MY GREAT GRANDMOTHER
(MY MOTHER'S MOTHER'S MOTHER)

NAME _____

BORN _____
DATE   PLACE

MARRIED _____
DATE   PLACE

DIED _____
DATE   PLACE

GENEALOGICAL DATA

MY BROTHERS AND SISTERS

NAME _____

BORN _____
      DATE   PLACE

MARRIED _____
          DATE   PLACE

DIED _____
     DATE   PLACE

NAME _____

BORN _____
      DATE   PLACE

MARRIED _____
          DATE   PLACE

DIED _____
     DATE   PLACE

NAME _____

BORN _____
      DATE   PLACE

MARRIED _____
          DATE   PLACE

DIED _____
     DATE   PLACE

NAME _____

BORN _____
      DATE   PLACE

MARRIED _____
          DATE   PLACE

DIED _____
     DATE   PLACE

MY FATHER'S BROTHERS AND SISTERS (MY AUNTS AND UNCLES)

NAME _____

BORN _____
      DATE   PLACE

MARRIED _____
          DATE   PLACE

DIED _____
     DATE   PLACE

NAME _____

BORN _____
      DATE   PLACE

MARRIED _____
          DATE   PLACE

DIED _____
     DATE   PLACE

NAME _____

BORN _____
      DATE   PLACE

MARRIED _____
          DATE   PLACE

DIED _____
     DATE   PLACE

NAME _____

BORN _____
      DATE   PLACE

MARRIED _____
          DATE   PLACE

DIED _____
     DATE   PLACE

MY FIRST COUSINS (FATHER'S SIDE)

NAME _____

BORN _____
      DATE   PLACE

MARRIED _____
          DATE   PLACE

DIED _____
     DATE   PLACE

NAME _____

BORN _____
      DATE   PLACE

MARRIED _____
          DATE   PLACE

DIED _____
     DATE   PLACE

Genealogists record the dates and places of birth, marriage and death for each member of the family. In the spaces below, fill in as many birth dates and places as you can. When appropriate, include dates and places of marriage and death.

NAME _____

BORN _____
       DATE   PLACE

MARRIED _____
       DATE   PLACE

DIED _____
       DATE   PLACE

NAME _____

BORN _____
       DATE   PLACE

MARRIED _____
       DATE   PLACE

DIED _____
       DATE   PLACE

MY MOTHER'S BROTHERS AND SISTERS (MY AUNTS AND UNCLES)

NAME _____

BORN _____
       DATE   PLACE

MARRIED _____
       DATE   PLACE

DIED _____
       DATE   PLACE

NAME _____

BORN _____
       DATE   PLACE

MARRIED _____
       DATE   PLACE

DIED _____
       DATE   PLACE

NAME _____

BORN _____
       DATE   PLACE

MARRIED _____
       DATE   PLACE

DIED _____
       DATE   PLACE

NAME _____

BORN _____
       DATE   PLACE

MARRIED _____
       DATE   PLACE

DIED _____
       DATE   PLACE

MY FIRST COUSINS (MOTHER'S SIDE)

NAME _____

BORN _____
       DATE   PLACE

MARRIED _____
       DATE   PLACE

DIED _____
       DATE   PLACE

NAME _____

BORN _____
       DATE   PLACE

MARRIED _____
       DATE   PLACE

DIED _____
       DATE   PLACE

NAME _____

BORN _____
       DATE   PLACE

MARRIED _____
       DATE   PLACE

DIED _____
       DATE   PLACE

NAME _____

BORN _____
       DATE   PLACE

MARRIED _____
       DATE   PLACE

DIED _____
       DATE   PLACE

ONE OF THE MOST INTERESTING KINDS OF FAMILY TREES IS ONE made of photographs. It is not an easy tree to "grow." Photography was not common until the late 1800's, and so it is often difficult to find photographs of our earlier ancestors. This is my Family Tree. It includes a picture of my brother and me, my parents, grandparents, great-grandparents, and even two of my great-great grandparents!

MY GREAT-GREAT GRANDPARENTS

Zsofi Fried and Samuel Grunberger. Mateszalka, Hungary, ca. 1870.

Avraham Abusch Kurzweil and Hinde Ruchel Lowenthal. Przemysl, Poland ca. 1885.

Ruchel Ennis. Dobromil, Poland, date unknown.

MY GREAT GRANDPARENTS

Hannah Grunberger and Marton Klein. Presov, Czechoslovakia, date unknown.

Blima Rath and Asher Yehoshia Gottlieb. Borgo Prund, Transylvania, ca. 1929.

MY GRANDPARENTS

Helen Klein. New York, ca. 1920.

Samuel L. Gottlieb.
Bistritz, Czechoslovakia, ca. 1929.

Mollie Ennis. Dobromil, Poland, ca. 1920.

Julius Kurzweil. New York City, ca. 1925.

MY PARENTS

Evelyn Gottlieb and Saul H. Kurzweil. East Meadow, New York, 1981.

MY BROTHERS, MY SISTERS AND ME

Ken Kurzweil and Arthur Kurzweil. East Meadow, New York, 1981.

My Family Tree

Find photographs of as many of your direct ancestors as possible. Mount copies of the photographs in the appropriate places. Label the photographs with the people's names, the place where the photo was taken, and the date if known. If you only know an approximate date, write "ca." and then the date. The "ca." means "approximately."

MY GREAT-GREAT GRANDPARENTS

MY GREAT GRANDPARENTS

MY GRANDPARENTS

MY PARENTS

MY BROTHERS, MY SISTERS AND ME

ZSUZSA BARTA IS MY SECOND COUSIN. SHE GREW UP IN Budapest, Hungary. Zsuzsa (Hungarian for Susan) and I are the same age. We met for the first time when we were twenty seven years old. Our grandmothers were sisters. My grandmother came to America when she was a teenager, but Zsuzsa's grandmother never left Hungary. When Zsuzsa and I met for the first time we felt as if we had known each other all our lives. Perhaps it was the fact that our "family ties" are close. We are second cousins, after all. Ever since we met during my first visit to Hungary we have felt a special closeness.

I took a photograph of Zsuzsa. When I returned home to New York, I had the photo developed and placed it in my family album. It was then that I noticed a photograph of my grandmother just a few pages from where I had placed the picture of Zsuzsa.

The photo of my grandmother was taken over sixty five years ago, but the similarity was remarkable!

My Family Look-Alikes

Some of the people in my family look more alike than others.

I look like _____

I have the same color hair as my _____

My eyes are like my _____

I am tall (short) like my _____

MY PICTURE

A PICTURE OF THE PERSON IN
MY FAMILY I LOOK MOST LIKE

AGE _____

DATE OF PHOTOGRAPH _____

NAME _____

RELATIONSHIP _____

DATE OF PHOTOGRAPH _____ 41

AGE IN PHOTOGRAPH _____

Languages in My Family

English is a new language for Jews. Your ancestors, just a few generations ago, probably did not speak English. Throughout the span of Jewish history, Jews have spoken many languages—Hebrew, Yiddish, Judezmo, Aramaic, and the national languages of the countries where they lived. What languages did your ancestors speak? What languages are spoken or read by the members of your family today?

NAME _____ RELATIONSHIP TO ME _____

LANGUAGES SPOKEN _____ LANGUAGES READ _____

NAME _____ RELATIONSHIP TO ME _____

LANGUAGES SPOKEN _____ LANGUAGES READ _____

NAME _____ RELATIONSHIP TO ME _____

LANGUAGES SPOKEN _____ LANGUAGES READ _____

NAME _____ RELATIONSHIP TO ME _____

LANGUAGES SPOKEN _____ LANGUAGES READ _____

CHAPTER 3
WHAT IS YOUR NAME?

What is your name?

That sounds like a foolish question. All of us know our own names. But in Jewish tradition, the question is not so foolish—and not so simple.

For example, you probably have at least two first names: an English name and a Hebrew name—unless your name is the biblical kind like David or Naomi and pretty much the same in both languages.

In some places you are called by your English name and in other places you are called by your Hebrew name. If you go to a public school, your English name is almost certainly used. In religious school, you are probably known by your Hebrew name. So you have two names already.

But you have another name as well—or at least a more *complete* name in Hebrew, and that is the name by which you are called to the Torah on your Bar or Bat Mitzvah day, the name which will be written on your ketubah when you get married. It is the name which links you to your parents. Your complete Hebrew name contains your first name, plus the word "ben", which means "son of" or "bat," which means "daughter of," and then your father's name. In the past, only the father's name was used, but now more and more Jews are using their father's name *and* their mother's name. After all, you are the child of *both* your parents.

Your name was probably someone else's name. One of the most popular customs in Jewish tradition is to name a baby after someone else. If your family is European (Ashkenazi) then tradition forbids the naming of a child after someone who is living. If you are from a Sephardi family, then naming a child after a living person is a permissible and common custom.

If most Jews are named after someone, that means you probably are too. Often, a Jew is named after a grandparent, great grandparent, or other relative. Sometimes, we are named after two different people.

Jews believe in the power of names. We believe that certain qualities come with a name. Think of it this way: there is a baseball team named the Detroit Tigers. Why are they named "Tigers" rather than "Kittens?" After all, both are cats. But, in order to have a name which best reflects a strong team, the name of the team is strong, too.

When a Jewish child is named after someone, we hope that the qualities of the person who originally had the name will be transmitted to the new baby. If you are named after a kind, honest, cheerful grandmother, your parents hoped that you too would be kind, honest, and cheerful.

What is your last name?

Again, it seems like a simple question, but there are some interesting things we can ask about your last name. For example, what is your mother's family name?

When I began to trace my family history, I discovered what many family historians and genealogists had already discovered: it's more difficult to trace the family of a female ancestor than that of a male one. This is because of our naming customs.

As a rule, children take their father's last name (also known as surname). This is because in most cases the mother of the child has already done the same. It is customary for a wife to take her husband's last name, although in recent years this has begun to change. Most of us know married women who have either kept their own last name or combined it with their husband's. Even a woman who does not use her husband's last name is still being partial to a male last name because she is probably using her *father's,* not her mother's. This can all get quite complicated.

The family historian often finds no record of the bride's original family name. Think of it this way: just because I have used the name KURZWEIL all of my life does not mean that I am *only* a KURZWEIL. My mother's name was GOTTLIEB before she married my father, so I am also a GOTTLIEB, just as much as a KURZWEIL. It does not end there, of course. In fact, with each additional generation more last names are added and the number of families you belong to increases. Remember, in just ten generations you have 1024 direct ancestors, and that reflects a lot of last names!

Jews did not always have last names. Last names were not necessary when Jews lived in small towns and had little contact with the outside world. Someone could be called simply Chaim ben Moshe or Chaim the Baker. But about two hundred years ago, European countries began requiring Jews to take last names if they did not already have them and to officially register their last names.

As you know, the late Golda Meir was a Prime Minister of Israel. That is the name she chose when, like many Israelis, she adopted a Hebrew last name. Before that, she was Golda Meyerson. And the first Prime Minister of Israel, David Ben-Gurion, grew up with the name David Green. Many Israelis have changed their European names to modern Hebrew names.

There is also an interesting example of a reversal of name changing. You may have heard of Irving Wallace. It is enough for our purposes to know that he is a well-known novelist and that he is Jewish. Well, Irving Wallace has a son who is also a writer. But his son's name is David Wallechinsky. David changed his name *back* to what it was originally before the family came to America.

Stories are told about Jews who, when they arrived in America, changed or shortened their last names. Rosenberg was changed to Rose, Cohen to Kane, and so on. There may be a story about your family's name for you to uncover!

My Names

MY FIRST NAME IS (English) _____

MY MIDDLE NAME IS _____

MY LAST NAME (Surname) IS _____

MY NICKNAME IS _____

MY COMPLETE HEBREW NAME IS _____

MY FATHER'S HEBREW NAME IS _____

MY MOTHER'S HEBREW NAME IS _____

MY FATHER'S FATHER'S HEBREW NAME IS _____

MY FATHER'S MOTHER'S HEBREW NAME IS _____

MY MOTHER'S FATHER'S HEBREW NAME IS _____

MY MOTHER'S MOTHER'S HEBREW NAME IS _____

MY MOTHER'S FAMILY NAME IS _____

MY FATHER'S MOTHER'S FAMILY NAME IS _____

MY MOTHER'S MOTHER'S FAMILY NAME IS _____

MY LAST NAME WAS CHANGED. THE ORIGINAL NAME WAS

_____

THE ORIGINAL NAME WAS CHANGED BECAUSE _____

_____

_____

_____

_____

_____

My NAMESAKE

We are named after people to remember. You are a living memorial to someone in your family, someone your parents wanted to remember. The person after whom you were named is called your namesake.

I WAS NAMED AFTER:

COMPLETE NAME (English) _____

COMPLETE NAME (Hebrew) _____

FAMILY RELATIONSHIP TO ME _____

PLACE OF RESIDENCE _____

OCCUPATION _____

Find out as much as you can about your namesake. Describe your namesake, including physical and personality characteristics. Perhaps there is a story you've been told about this person. Record it here.

_____

_____

_____

_____

_____

If you can find a photograph of your namesake, mount copy here.

MY NAMESAKE

You may be able to discover the person who had your name even earlier than your namesake. Who was your namesake's namesake?

_____

My Relatives' Namesakes

Record the names of your closest relatives and find out after whom they were named. In the spaces marked THEIR RELATIONSHIP describe how the two people are related to one another.

FATHER

ENGLISH NAME _____

HEBREW NAME _____

HIS NAMESAKE _____

THEIR RELATIONSHIP _____

MOTHER

ENGLISH NAME _____

HEBREW NAME _____

HER NAMESAKE _____

THEIR RELATIONSHIP _____

OTHER RELATIVES

ENGLISH NAME _____

HEBREW NAME _____

NAMESAKE _____

THEIR RELATIONSHIP _____

ENGLISH NAME _____

HEBREW NAME _____

NAMESAKE _____

THEIR RELATIONSHIP _____

BROTHERS AND SISTERS

ENGLISH NAME _____

HEBREW NAME _____

NAMESAKE _____

THEIR RELATIONSHIP _____

ENGLISH NAME _____

HEBREW NAME _____

NAMESAKE _____

THEIR RELATIONSHIP _____

ENGLISH NAME _____

HEBREW NAME _____

NAMESAKE _____

THEIR RELATIONSHIP _____

ENGLISH NAME _____

HEBREW NAME _____

NAMESAKE _____

THEIR RELATIONSHIP _____

Family Signatures

Autograph collecting is a popular hobby. And when you get samples of the signatures of your own family members, your collection will be that much more personal and special. (Begin with your parents, brothers and sisters, grandparents, and don't forget your aunts, uncles and cousins.)

PERSON'S NAME (print)	RELATIONSHIP	SIGNATURE	DATE

CHAPTER 4
WHAT DO YOU EAT?

The old piece of paper was torn and stained from previous years of spilled milk, splashed eggs, and dried flour. On the paper you could read the recipe my mother had written years earlier as she watched her mother-in-law make delicious blintzes.

Although my grandmother died over twenty five years ago, my mother still makes the same recipe each year from that same piece of paper. And I have since copied the recipe, and I make the blintzes in my home as well.

As a young child, I used to watch my mother prepare this recipe. Each year she would use the same piece of paper, the same cooking utensils, and I would wait anxiously until she was finished. For then I was allowed to lick the bowl in which the sweet cheese mixture was prepared. It, too, was delicious.

My grandmother learned this recipe from her mother. I, in turn, learned it from my mother, making the recipe at least four generations old. I will never prepare that recipe without thinking about my mother and my grandmother. In fact, I never eat blintzes anywhere without thinking about them.

One of the first things we learn from our parents is how and what to eat. The kinds of foods we develop a taste for are those our parents exposed us to. In turn, our parents learned these tastes from their parents, and so on. Many of the things you like to eat are probably things that your great-grandparents liked too.

There may be third generation recipes in your family. And if your grandparents learned to cook from their parents, as they probably did, there are even fourth generation or fifth generation recipes that you still enjoy today.

These recipes are history. Part of who we are has to do with the food we eat. Italian food is very different from Chinese food which is very different from Jewish food. And there are differences that depend on where these foods originally came from. There is northern Italian food and food from the south of Italy; Cantonese food from China and Mandarin food from China; Jewish food from Eastern Europe and Jewish food from the Sephardic Jewish communities of Greece, Turkey and North Africa. Every culture has its own special ways of cooking.

There are special food customs associated with our holidays. Sometimes they are more complex than other times. A holiday like Pesah, for example, is filled with special foods and food customs. Shavuot, on the other hand, has simpler customs relating to the kinds of foods traditionally eaten.

Recipes connect the generations. Think about the foods we eat during the Passover holiday. These foods have been eaten by Jews throughout the world for generations. They used recipes similar to those we use. Surely their matzah was not quite as nice and neat as the machine-made ones we buy, but the formula—the recipe—is the same. Haroset, that tasty mixture of nuts, apples and wine is a combination of ingredients passed down from generation to generation.

What is a Jewish dish? Actually, many of the dishes we call "Jewish" are not really "Jewish" at all. At least they are not exclusively Jewish. Dishes which our ancestors brought with them from Eastern Europe and Russia were very typical food in those regions of the world. They were eaten by everyone living there. We think of them as Jewish dishes because they are different from the foods eaten by our non-Jewish friends today. If you have ever seen the menu of a Russian restaurant you might think you were looking at the menu of a Jewish restaurant. In some cases the names of the dishes might be different, but the food will look and often taste the same.

There is one thing about food which is unique to Jewish culture and experience and that is the kosher laws—the laws of kashrut. In the Torah, and further explained in the Talmud and other classic Jewish texts, there are a set of practices detailing with the ways we can and cannot prepare foods, and listing the foods we can and cannot eat.

Jewish family history is, in some ways, like a ride on a roller coaster. In one generation everyone may be Orthodox, and two generations later, in that same family, people may not be observant at all. Let me illustrate by exploring one branch of my own family tree.

My great-great-great-grandfather was a Hasidic rabbi in Eastern Europe. He was a strictly observant Jew. His daughter was the wife of a rabbi and was probably as observant as her father. Her son (my great-grandfather) was also a rabbi and an observant Jew, but his children were not. They left home and scattered around the world. One of his children, my grandfather, came to America at the age of seventeen. He and his daughter (my mother) chose not to observe the laws of kashrut. Finally we come down to me—and I am closer to my great-great-great-grandfather concerning my observance of kashrut. So you can see the "roller coaster" I was talking about.

FAVORITE HOLIDAY FOODS

_____

_____

_____

_____

_____

_____

_____

_____

_____

_____

_____

_____

_____

_____

_____

_____

_____

_____

_____

_____

_____

51

The synagogue of Mateszalka, Hungary

Matzah-making machine

ON PASSOVER, WE READ FROM THE HAGGADAH, "IN EVERY GEN-eration, each person must regard it as if he *himself* has come out of Egypt." At the Passover seder, we repeat the same ancient customs that were performed by our ancestors for centuries. One of those customs is eating matzah—the un-leavened bread. When we eat matzah, we share an experience with Jews throughout the world. In each and every generation, through an unbroken chain, we unite with our ancestors by repeating the very same ritual. Through the simple act of eating unleavened bread, we share in the history of the Jewish People.

I once traveled to the town of Mateszalka in Hungary. My grandmother, Helen Gottlieb, had lived there as a child. There is no longer a Jewish community in Mateszalka, but I did locate the old, abandoned synagogue. I went inside to investigate. Among the things I found, was a odd-looking machine standing in the corner of the synagogue's cellar. It was a matzah-making machine. My grandmother had lived in that town. My great grandparents had lived in that town too. My great-great grandparents had probably also lived there. Certainly my ancestors had eaten matzah made on that very machine!

FAMILY RECIPE

THIS IS A RECIPE FOR _____

THE RECIPE WAS GIVEN TO ME BY _____

WHO LEARNED IT FROM _____

PLACE OF ORIGIN _____

THE RECIPE HAS BEEN IN MY FAMILY FOR _____ YEARS.

INGREDIENTS:

DIRECTIONS:

A SPECIAL FAMILY STORY CONNECTED TO THIS DISH: _____

_____

_____

_____

_____

MY MOTHER TAUGHT ME TO PREPARE A DISH WHICH HER mother-in-law taught her. She, in turn, was taught by her mother. So the recipe is at least four generations old now—and probably older! But this recipe calls for "one glass of milk." No recipe today would say that. It might say 8 ounces of milk, or 6 ounces of milk, or one cup of milk. But when my mother was taught this recipe by my grandmother, the family did not own a measuring cup. Instead, they used a glass. The question, of course, is what size was this glass? It would be easy to solve this problem if my grandmother were still alive—I would just ask her. But because she is no longer living, the riddle must be solved in a different way.

The clue lies in knowing something about Jewish ritual. It is traditional to burn a candle for an entire day on the anniversary of the death of a loved one. This candle is called a "yahrzeit" candle. These memorial candles come in a glass—always the same size glass, since the candle must last for the same length of time. And, since my grandmother came from a poor family, unable to buy a special set of drinking glasses, she, like many other poor Jews, used yahrzeit glasses in her kitchen—for drinking, and for measuring. And that's how much milk is in "one glass of milk"—just enough to fill a yahrzeit glass!

Family Recipe

THIS IS A RECIPE FOR _____

THE RECIPE WAS GIVEN TO ME BY _____

WHO LEARNED IT FROM _____

PLACE OF ORIGIN _____

THE RECIPE HAS BEEN IN MY FAMILY FOR _____ YEARS.

INGREDIENTS:

DIRECTIONS:

A SPECIAL FAMILY STORY CONNECTED TO THIS DISH: _____

_____

_____

_____

_____

55

Family Recipe

THIS IS A RECIPE FOR _____

THE RECIPE WAS GIVEN TO ME BY _____

WHO LEARNED IT FROM _____

PLACE OF ORIGIN _____

THE RECIPE HAS BEEN IN MY FAMILY FOR _____ YEARS.

INGREDIENTS:

DIRECTIONS:

A SPECIAL FAMILY STORY CONNECTED TO THIS DISH: _____

_____

_____

_____

_____

ONE SUMMER, I WAS HIRED AS THE COOK IN A NEW HAMPSHIRE
camp. Feeling quite ambitious, I decided to prepare my family's blintzes recipe for everyone. The population of the camp was 60. I cooked all night, making over 120 blintzes. And during the middle of the night, when the camp was
silent and still, I could feel the presence of my grandmother, who died when I
was six. Through her recipe, I was connected to my past that night, in a mys-
terious way that I shall never forget.

Family Recipe

THIS IS A RECIPE FOR _____

THE RECIPE WAS GIVEN TO ME BY _____

WHO LEARNED IT FROM _____

PLACE OF ORIGIN _____

THE RECIPE HAS BEEN IN MY FAMILY FOR _____ YEARS.

INGREDIENTS:

DIRECTIONS:

A SPECIAL FAMILY STORY CONNECTED TO THIS DISH: _____

_____

_____

_____

_____

CHAPTER 5
YOUR MOST IMPORTANT POSSESSIONS

Most of us have funny relationships with objects. We save our money for months, hoping to buy a certain expensive item that we've had our eye on for a long time, and then, when we finally buy it, it either isn't what we thought it would be, or within a short time we get tired of it.

With a little bit of thought, we can begin to put together the story of our relationship to some objects. You probably know the most expensive thing you own. And with just a little figuring, you can probably find the oldest thing in your possession.

Since most Jewish families in the United States arrived here within the last 100 years, almost all of our families had to make important decisions about *objects* very recently in history. Even objects which cost a lot of money or which were in the family for generations, may have been left behind. Immigrants could bring only a bare minimum with them to America.

When I look around my home, trying to decide what few objects I might attempt to take with me under such circumstances, I look first at my books. I have hundreds of books; I could not possibly take many of them. On the other hand, almost all of my books are replaceable. There are only a few rare and valuable items in my book collection which would be difficult to replace. So, books would not be my first choice.

I then look at my family photographs, knowing that these are priceless and in many cases "one of a kind," and I know that the photos would surely be among the few things I would take with me anywhere.

The oldest family objects I have are photographs taken in Europe. In fact, of all the things in my family's possession, I believe the photographs are the oldest. And this, of course, makes sense, because photographs are probably the easiest things to keep. When my ancestors came to America, they couldn't bring much with them—but photos were simple enough to carry.

In the same way that the family photos are irreplaceable, so too are some of the ritual objects which I have received from family members.

Each Hanukkah, for example, I light the Hanukkah menorah that once belonged to my mother's father. I don't know how long he had it nor how old it is, but this does not matter. What does matter to me is that it was *his*. It is not just *any* menorah. I have seen bigger ones, more beautiful ones, and more valuable ones, but none is more valuable to me than the one given to me by one of my grandfathers—the one *he* used during most of his life. I would have a very difficult time giving up that Hanukkah menorah.

When I asked my father what he has in his possession that belonged to *his* father (who died almost 20 years ago) I was shown a set of tefillin which my grandfather used during his lifetime.

Jewish tradition is rich with things to help make Jewish life more meaningful and rewarding.

16th century silver spice box.

Pewter Hanukkah lamp.

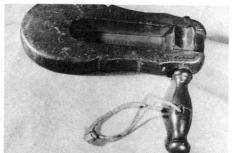

19th century Russian Purim gragger.

Silver etrog box.

Traditional Sabbath candlesticks and cup.

Seder plate, Haggadah and Cup of Elijah.

JEWS HAVE ALWAYS RECOGNIZED THE POWER OF FAMILY
heirlooms. In a special way, the old and cherished objects we save connect us to
our history. Like wine in a bottle, they grow richer with age. These precious
objects carry with them a history that often adds meaning to our lives.

Many of our holidays and customs require ritual objects. These objects are often kept in the family from generation to generation. It is possible that there are old ritual objects in your family's possession. Some may still be used. Some may be stored away in your house or in the home of a relative. Somewhere there is probably a Jewish ritual object waiting to be found. Perhaps the greatest value of your detective work is to find a Jewish ritual object no longer being used—and use it! Here are some items to look for: candlesticks, kiddush cup, tallit, tefillin, kippot, menorah, spice box, tzedakah box. What have you found?

Family HEIRLOOMS

NAME OF ITEM _____

LOCATION _____

MADE OF _____

APPROXIMATE AGE _____

USED FOR _____

ORIGINALLY BELONGED TO _____

_____

ORIGINALLY CAME FROM _____

_____

NAME OF ITEM _____

LOCATION _____

MADE OF _____

APPROXIMATE AGE _____

USED FOR _____

ORIGINALLY BELONGED TO _____

_____

ORIGINALLY CAME FROM _____

_____

NAME OF ITEM _____

LOCATION _____

MADE OF _____

APPROXIMATE AGE _____

USED FOR _____

ORIGINALLY BELONGED TO _____

_____

ORIGINALLY CAME FROM _____

_____

NAME OF ITEM _____

LOCATION _____

MADE OF _____

APPROXIMATE AGE _____

USED FOR _____

ORIGINALLY BELONGED TO _____

_____

ORIGINALLY CAME FROM _____

_____

I ONCE HAD SOME PRIVATE CONVERSATIONS WITH ELIE WIESEL, the well-known Jewish writer. At our first meeting, I was prepared to ask him many questions. To my surprise, he asked me a question first. Elie Wiesel asked "What is your earliest Jewish memory?"

I sat silently for a few moments. Suddenly, a scene appeared before me. I was sitting on my grandfather's lap. We were in his small synagogue in Brooklyn, New York. It was Rosh Hashanah. I was only four years old, but I can clearly recall, as if it were yesterday, my grandfather and me wrapped together in his large tallit. The tallit created a warm, cozy tent for us; the soft fabric rubbed gently on my face as my grandfather held me tight. And every once in a while, my grandfather would tease me, or whisper something funny in my ear.

I could see the rabbi standing in the center of the synagogue on the raised platform (the *bimah*). As my memory wandered back to that early moment in my Jewish experience, I recalled the sound of the shofar being blown. I remembered the tears on the rabbi's face.

Elie Wiesel listened to my memory and then asked me, "Do you know why we blow the shofar on Rosh Hashanah? Our sages tell us that the sound of the shofar wakes us up. It wakes us up to remember."

And he was right. Every time I hear the sound of the shofar I remember that long ago day in my grandfather's synagogue. And every time I feel my tallit wrapped around me as I pray, I remember my grandfather's tallit, as it held us both—on the first day of the year, the first day of Creation, the first memory I have . . . as a Jew.

Books are often among the oldest possessions in a household. Make an inventory of your family's oldest books, directing your attention first to the Jewish books you have. What are the three oldest Jewish books in your home? If you are unable to locate any old Jewish books, look for other old books in your family library.

OUR OLDEST BOOKS

TITLE _____

AUTHOR _____

DATE OF PUBLICATION _____

PLACE OF PUBLICATION _____

SUBJECT _____

LANGUAGE _____

ORIGINALLY BELONGED TO _____

_____

TITLE _____

AUTHOR _____

DATE OF PUBLICATION _____

PLACE OF PUBLICATION _____

SUBJECT _____

LANGUAGE _____

ORIGINALLY BELONGED TO _____

TITLE _____

AUTHOR _____

DATE OF PUBLICATION _____

PLACE OF PUBLICATION _____

SUBJECT _____

LANGUAGE _____

ORIGINALLY BELONGED TO _____

_____

TITLE _____

AUTHOR _____

DATE OF PUBLICATION _____

PLACE OF PUBLICATION _____

SUBJECT _____

LANGUAGE _____

ORIGINALLY BELONGED TO _____

THE TWENTY ONE PEOPLE IN THIS PHOTOGRAPH ARE ALL members of the Kurzweil family. The picture was taken in Dobromil, Poland in the year 1926.

Let me introduce you to the people in the picture.

The man with the beard, sitting in the middle of the photograph, is Avrum Abusch Kurzweil, the head of the family. Though his name was Avrum Abusch, he was known to everyone as Abusch. Abusch's wife was not alive when the photograph was taken. She died in 1915.

The man standing at the upper left corner is a son of Abusch's named Eli. His wife, Dobroh, is seated in front of him along with their three children — Gershom, Hinde Ruchel and a baby whose name I do not know.

The next man in the back row is Hersh, another son of Abusch. His wife, Anna, is seated in front of him with their four children—Isaac, Mosh, Shmil, and Mechel.

The man, standing in the middle of the back row, is Sam, the youngest child of Abusch. He is not married in this photograph; he's seventeen years old. Sam married several years later in America.

The woman next to Sam, standing in the back row, is my grandmother, Mollie. Her husband (my grandfather) is not in this picture. He was in America earning money to bring over his wife and three children. The three children are in the photograph. One is the boy holding the violin. The boy's name is Ray. Another is the girl on Abusch's lap. Her name is Ruth. And the third is the boy sitting in the front row below Abusch. That's Saul. He's my father.

The woman sitting on the right side of the photograph is Raisl, daughter of Abusch. Her husband, Shimon, is standing behind her. They have two children. One is Temma, sitting on her mother's lap. The other is Beille, sitting right below the violin.

That's the Kurzweil family in Dobromil. Of the twenty one family members in this photograph, fourteen were murdered during the Holocaust.

Family Photographs

Use these pages to mount copies of your favorite family photographs. Under each picture, write the location, date and event and then list the people in the photograph.

66

WHEN I WAS GROWING UP I HAD WHAT I CALLED A "JUNK drawer." I stuffed all the little things I didn't want to throw away into this dresser drawer—letters, parts of toys, baseball cards, balls of string. I still have a drawer in my desk where I keep stuffing little things I don't want to part with. You too might have this kind of drawer.

When my grandparents decided to move from their apartment in New York after forty years, I was asked to help with the packing. It sounded like quite a chore. But to my surpise, packing day became a day of discovery. I found that my grandmother also had a "junk drawer." And in that drawer I discovered this telegram.

The telegram, addressed to my grandmother, Helen Gottlieb, seems senseless. It hardly has any information on it, but it illustrates how one little piece of paper can represent far more than one might think at first. It tells a story worth repeating.

My grandmother had come to America from Hungary when she was a teenager. She came with her sister, leaving several members of her family in various cities in Hungary. Some members of her family came to America later, but one sister, Szeren, stayed in Europe and married a man whose last name was Breuer.

During the Holocaust, many members of my grandmother's family were murdered. Like many Jews in the United States and elsewhere in the world, my grandmother made inquiry through the United States Government to see if any information could be obtained about possible surviving relatives. Lists of Survivors were published, and, on the basis of those lists, aid was sent to help those relatives who miraculously survived. My grandmother's sister, Szeren, was one of those Survivors.

This telegram was the first message sent to my grandmother by her sister. It contains only a few words. It looks like just another scrap of paper. But it reflects an important moment in my family's history. I can only imagine the joy that my grandmother felt when this telegram arrived . . . when she learned that her sister had survived!

CLASS OF SERVICE		SYMBOLS
This is a full-rate Telegram or Cablegram unless its deferred character is indicated by a suitable symbol above or preceding the address.	**WESTERN UNION** 1201 A. N. WILLIAMS PRESIDENT	DL = Day Letter
		NL = Night Letter
		LC = Deferred Cable
		NLT = Cable Night Letter
		Ship Radiogram

The filing time shown in the date line on telegrams and day letters is STANDARD TIME at point of origin. Time of receipt is STANDARD TIME at point of destination

M31CC JG INTL

        CD BUDAPEST VIA MACKA RDO 27 5

NLT GOTTLIEB

        HELEN 1557 GRAND CONCOURSE APT 33D NEWYORK 5? USA (END)

HAD US AID PERHAPS TROUGH THE AMERICAN MISSION OF BUDAPEST

MUCH LOVE YOUR SISTER

                BREUER SZEREN

                304A NOV 7

Family Documents

Family historians collect stories, photographs, names, books and important personal documents. While it is best to collect the originals or at least good copies of documents, sometimes the best you can do is to record the location of a document.

DOCUMENT

LOCATION

DOCUMENT

LOCATION

DOCUMENT

LOCATION

DOCUMENT

LOCATION

DOCUMENT

LOCATION

DOCUMENT

LOCATION

DOCUMENT

LOCATION

DOCUMENT

LOCATION

UNITED STATES OF AMERICA

CERTIFICATE OF CITIZENSHIP

No. 3889298

TO BE GIVEN TO
THE PERSON NATURALIZED

Petition No. 242620

Personal description of holder as of date of naturalization: Age 67 years; sex male; color white; complexion dark; color of eyes brown; color of hair brown-grayish; height 5 feet 2 inches; weight 160 pounds; visible distinctive marks none; Marital status Married; former nationality Poland Austria.

I certify that the description given is true, and that the photograph affixed hereto is a likeness of me.

ORIGINAL

Abusoh Kurzweil

(Complete and true signature of holder)

UNITED STATES OF AMERICA
SOUTHERN DISTRICT OF NEW YORK } ss.

Be it known that Abusoh Kurzweil then residing at 65 Cannon Street New York City District of The United States

having petitioned to be admitted a citizen of the United States of America, and at a term of the court having first

New York City on May 20th 1935

held pursuant to law at

The court having found that the petitioner intends to reside permanently in the United States, had in all respects complied with the Naturalization Laws of the United States in such case applicable, and was entitled to be so admitted, the court thereupon ordered that the petitioner be admitted as a citizen of the United States of America.

In testimony whereof the seal of the court is hereunto affixed this 20th day of May in the year of our Lord nineteen hundred and 35 and of our Independence the one hundred and 59th.

Charles Weiser.

George A. U.S. District Court.

By _____ Deputy Clerk.

Seal

DEPARTMENT OF LABOR

Citizenship Certificate of Author's Great Grandfather

Family Documents

If you are lucky enough to have original documents, treat them carefully. If they are folded, the best thing to do is to unfold them and store them that way. A folded document gets opened and closed so many times that, over the years, it begins to crack or tear. Kept open, an old document will last much longer. Keep the originals you gather in a safe place, but first take the time to photocopy them. The general rule is always have more than just one copy of something of value. For your family record, make copies of some of the more important or interesting documents and papers and mount them here.

Documents

MANY RABBIS ARE DISCUSSED IN THE TALMUD. MY FAVORITE is Nakhum Gamzu. Nakhum was always an optimist. He always saw the potential for good. His name, "Gamzu," was taken from the saying he often spoke: "*Gam zu* l'tova" (*This too* is for good!)

One of my favorite sayings is: "See the glass half full, not half empty." I don't remember when I first heard this saying, but I have been moved by its wisdom ever since. A half-filled glass is neither half full nor half empty. But *seeing* the glass half-full, rather than half empty, is a more positive way of looking at the world.

People are known for the things they say and repeat. Often, as I was growing up, I heard my mother say: "If you have nothing nice to say, don't say anything at all." The wisdom of *Silence* is a traditional Jewish belief. My mother, by the way, is known not only for the saying, but also as a living example of it.

Throughout history people have become identified with words they have spoken or written. President John F. Kennedy is remembered for: "Ask not what your country can do for you; ask what you can do for your country." Theodor Herzl's saying: "If you will it, it is no dream," has also become well known.

Brief statements or sayings are not new to the Jewish people. A whole book of the Bible, the Book of Proverbs, is devoted to short *words of wisdom* passed down through the ages. Our ancestors have always been interested in the wisdom to be found in words.

There are different kinds of sayings. Some have no known author. My father often says: "Even a broken clock is right twice a day." He didn't invent the phrase, but he finds it useful and has repeated it many times. I, too, have used the expression, but when I have, I say: "As my father often says, 'Even a broken clock is right twice a day.'" Our Jewish sages have taught that if you know the source of the words you speak, you should include them.

When my father thinks of his mother and grandfather, the Yiddish words: "*Mit Got's help*" (With God's help) come to mind. This traditional expression was often on the lips of my grandmother and my great grandfather. Similarly, the Hebrew expression, "Im irtza Ha-Shem" (May it be God's will) is frequently heard in the household of my wife and myself.

SAYINGS FROM THE TALMUD

More people die from overeating than from hunger.
SHABBAT 33a

One's name has an influence on one's life.
TALMUD, BERACHOT, 7b

God created Adam rather than creating the whole human race together for the sake of peace among mankind, so that no one could say, "My ancestor was greater than your ancestor.
MISHNAH, SANHEDRIN 4:5

Whoever teaches his son teaches not only his son but also his son's son—and so on to the end of generations. TALMUD, KIDDUSHIN, 30a

Can you remember an expression or proverb you associate with someone in your family? Perhaps your parents recall favorite sayings of their parents or grandparents. See how many family sayings you can collect and record.

Family Sayings

MY MOTHER'S

_____

_____

_____

MY FATHER'S

_____

_____

_____

MY GRANDFATHER'S (FATHER'S FATHER)

_____

_____

_____

MY GRANDMOTHER'S (FATHER'S MOTHER)

_____

_____

_____

MY GRANDFATHER'S (MOTHER'S FATHER)

_____

_____

_____

MY GRANDMOTHER'S (MOTHER'S MOTHER)

_____

_____

_____

MINE

_____

_____

_____

(OTHER)

_____

_____

_____

FAVORITE FAMILY STORIES

A family story need not be long. Just a few words can recall a moment of family history. This is one of my family's stories: In 1929, when my father was seven years old, he journeyed to America with his mother. brother and sister. On the ship that brought them here, a drunken sailor picked my father up and pretended to throw him overboard. The sailor was stopped, but nobody in the family ever forgot the incident. This ''family story'' has been told and retold many times by my father. Can you think of family stories to record here? If possible, record one story from your parents' generation, one from your grand-parents' generation, and one even further back than that.

_____

_____

_____

_____

_____

_____

_____

_____

_____

_____

_____

_____

_____

_____

_____

_____

_____

_____

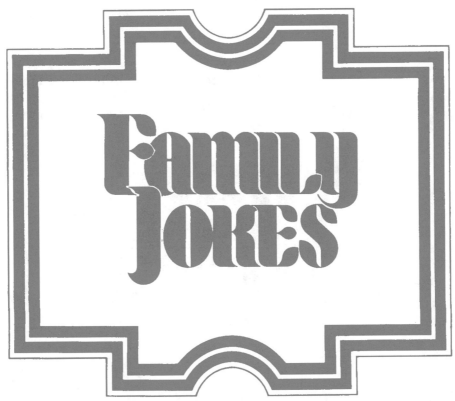

FAMILY JOKES

Jews have a long tradition of an appreciation for humor. In the earliest Jewish writings, we find examples of the power of humor. The Talmud teaches that humor is important and some rabbis were known for the funny stories they shared with their students. One Talmudic sage, Rabbi Huna, was known for beginning his classes with an amusing tale.

Families often share "family jokes." These funny stories are well known to the members of a household. Do you have family jokes in your home? Do you have any favorites? Perhaps your parents or grandparents have favorite jokes to share. Use this page to record the humorous stories told by members of your family.

_____

_____

_____

_____

_____

_____

_____

_____

_____

_____

_____

_____

Pets are often beloved members of a household. We often recall periods in our lives by the pets we had at a certain time. And in Jewish tradition, the Torah itself teaches us to be compassionate towards all animals.

NAME

BREED OR DESCRIPTION	FROM	UNTIL

MEMORIES

NAME

BREED OR DESCRIPTION	FROM	UNTIL

MEMORIES

NAME

BREED OR DESCRIPTION	FROM	UNTIL

MEMORIES

NAME

BREED OR DESCRIPTION	FROM	UNTIL

MEMORIES

CHAPTER 6
BECOMING A BAR/BAT MITZVAH

In the Hebrew School I attended everything I did was in preparation for my Bar Mitzvah. My Bar Mitzvah was the day I longed for, the day I would suddenly be . . . a "man"?

No. In *no way* was I treated like a "grown-up." When the day of my Bar Mitzvah came and went, I may have been a little richer from the gifts I received. I may have been delighted to be finished with my Bar Mitzvah lessons. But I was in no way the adult which the Bar Mitzvah was supposed to make me.

Looking back on my Bar Mitzvah and the Bar Mitzvahs of my friends, I recall that the most important aspect of the Bar Mitzvah plans was the party. Where would the party be? Who would be invited? What would I wear?

As it happened, I never had a "catered affair." My grandfather died two months before my Bar Mitzvah. While I still had a Bar Mitzvah in the synagogue, the festive party was cancelled.

My grandfather's death changed my Bar Mitzvah day radically. I had the sense that I was "replacing" him. I never shared this feeling with anyone on the day of my Bar Mitzvah or even soon after. I didn't know quite *how* to express my feelings about the subject, so I simply kept them to myself. But while I was sitting in the front of the synagogue, waiting nervously to get through with my part, I thought that perhaps there was a connection between my grandfather's passing and my "becoming a man."

My grandfather's absence was conspicuous. He was the most religious member of the family, and his influence on me was significant. So I believed that his death was a signal to me that I would be taking his place—as a Jew.

There was another feeling that I remember having on the day of my Bar Mitzvah: I had the vivid sense that I was repeating a custom which my father had performed and that his father had performed, and that *his* father had performed before him. My Bar Mitzvah was one more in a long chain of Bar Mitzvahs.

The Bar and Bat Mitzvah are a point in time when a Jewish boy and girl become responsible for themselves in the eyes of God. It is a "coming of age ceremony" quite unlike those of other people. For Jews, becoming an adult means added responsibilities and added learning. How do we celebrate our full participation as Jews?

By studying and reading the Torah.

My Bar / Bat Mitzvah

There is no mitzvah greater than the study of Torah. It is, therefore, no surprise that a first *aliyah*, being called to read publicly from the Torah for the first time, is considered a perfect way to mark a Bar and Bat Mitzvah.

What is the portion of the Torah for the day of your Bar/Bat Mitzvah?

THE NAME OF MY TORAH PORTION IS _____

IT IS IN THE BOOK _____

CHAPTER _____

LINES _____

_____

MY TORAH PORTION IS ABOUT _____

_____

_____

THE NAME OF MY HAFTORAH PORTION IS _____

IT IS IN THE BOOK _____

CHAPTER _____

LINES _____

MY HAFTORAH PORTION IS ABOUT _____

_____

THE DATE OF MY BAR/BAT MITZVAH _____ 19____

_____ 57____

Complete this record for your immediate family. Include your brothers and sisters, your parents and grandparents.

Family Bar/Bat Mitzvah Record

NAME _____ RELATIONSHIP _____

DATE _____ SYNAGOGUE _____

RABBI _____ CANTOR _____ TORAH PORTION _____

NAME _____ RELATIONSHIP _____

DATE _____ SYNAGOGUE _____

RABBI _____ CANTOR _____ TORAH PORTION _____

NAME _____ RELATIONSHIP _____

DATE _____ SYNAGOGUE _____

RABBI _____ CANTOR _____ TORAH PORTION _____

NAME _____ RELATIONSHIP _____

DATE _____ SYNAGOGUE _____

RABBI _____ CANTOR _____ TORAH PORTION _____

NAME _____ RELATIONSHIP _____

DATE _____ SYNAGOGUE _____

RABBI _____ CANTOR _____ TORAH PORTION _____

NAME _____ RELATIONSHIP _____

DATE _____ SYNAGOGUE _____

RABBI _____ CANTOR _____ TORAH PORTION _____

My Bar/Bat Mitzvah Speech

_____

_____

_____

_____

_____

_____

_____

_____

_____

_____

_____

_____

_____

_____

_____

_____

_____

_____

_____

_____

My TEACHERS

In Jewish tradition, the relationship between a teacher and a student has always been considered profoundly important. Consider first the people who taught you in school. But there have also been many others who help you learn important things. Who have your most important teachers been?

NAME OF TEACHER	SUBJECT	PLACE	DATES

When we prepare for our Bar or Bat Mitzvah, there is usually one person who takes on most of the responsibility for helping us to prepare. In my case, that person is

_____

NAME

ONE OF MY FAVORITE PHOTOGRAPHS IS A PICTURE OF MY father on the day of his Bar Mitzvah in 1935. The picture was taken on the roof of their apartment building in Brooklyn, New York.

My Family Bar/Bat Mitzvah Photographs

THIS PHOTO WAS TAKEN AT THE BAR/BAT MITZVAH OF _____

LOCATION _____ DATE _____

PEOPLE IN THE PICTURE ARE _____

THIS PHOTO WAS TAKEN AT THE BAR/BAT MITZVAH OF _____

LOCATION _____ DATE _____

PEOPLE IN THE PICTURE ARE _____

THIS PHOTO WAS TAKEN AT THE BAR/BAT MITZVAH OF

LOCATION   DATE

PEOPLE IN THE PICTURE ARE

THIS PHOTO WAS TAKEN AT THE BAR/BAT MITZVAH OF

LOCATION   DATE

PEOPLE IN THE PICTURE ARE

Family EDUCATION Record

MOTHER

ELEMENTARY SCHOOL		DATES
HIGH SCHOOL		DATES
RELIGIOUS SCHOOLS		DATES
COLLEGE	DEGREE	DATES
POST-GRADUATE	DEGREE	DATES

FATHER

ELEMENTARY SCHOOL		DATES
HIGH SCHOOL		DATES
RELIGIOUS SCHOOLS		DATES
COLLEGE	DEGREE	DATES
POST-GRADUATE	DEGREE	DATES

ME

ELEMENTARY SCHOOL		DATES
HIGH SCHOOL		DATES
RELIGIOUS SCHOOLS		DATES
COLLEGE	DEGREE	DATES
POST-GRADUATE	DEGREE	DATES

GRANDMOTHER (Mother's mother)

ELEMENTARY SCHOOL		DATES
HIGH SCHOOL		DATES
RELIGIOUS SCHOOLS		DATES
COLLEGE	DEGREE	DATES
POST-GRADUATE	DEGREE	DATES

GRANDFATHER (Mother's father)

ELEMENTARY SCHOOL		DATES
HIGH SCHOOL		DATES
RELIGIOUS SCHOOLS		DATES
COLLEGE	DEGREE	DATES
POST-GRADUATE	DEGREE	DATES

GRANDMOTHER (Father's mother)

ELEMENTARY SCHOOL		DATES
HIGH SCHOOL		DATES
RELIGIOUS SCHOOLS		DATES
COLLEGE	DEGREE	DATES
POST-GRADUATE	DEGREE	DATES

GRANDFATHER (Father's father)

ELEMENTARY SCHOOL		DATES
HIGH SCHOOL		DATES
RELIGIOUS SCHOOLS		DATES
COLLEGE	DEGREE	DATES
POST-GRADUATE	DEGREE	DATES

Family Synagogue Memberships

NAME OF SYNAGOGUE

ADDRESS

RABBI

CANTOR

YEARS OF AFFILIATION

NAME OF SYNAGOGUE

ADDRESS

RABBI

CANTOR

YEARS OF AFFILIATION

NAME OF SYNAGOGUE

ADDRESS

RABBI

CANTOR

YEARS OF AFFILIATION

Chapter 7
WHAT ARE YOU GOING TO BE?

"What are you going to be when you grow up?"

I was asked that question many times when I was in school. I suppose it is a common question.

I had a large selection of careers to pick from, and I never thought twice about any career being out of my reach.

But just two generations ago, that choice was not a part of my family history. My father's father was a tinsmith—and his father was a tinsmith too. In fact, my grandfather learned a trade from my great grandfather, and continued working for him until he started his own business. While I am not certain, my great-great grandfather was probably also a tinsmith. Three generations; one profession.

It was different for my other grandfather. He came to America as a young man of 17. He came here alone. Until he settled down to spend most of his life running a jewelry store, he went from job to job in this country, going back and forth between being a salesman and being a dance teacher. Sometimes he was also a diamond cutter. He was in a different world from his father, who was a rabbi. And *his* father was a rabbi, and *his* father was a rabbi, too.

The luxury of being able to select your own career is a recent one. Of course, we all know some people who follow the same occupation as their parents. But in most cases they choose a different one.

If your family was like most in Eastern Europe, your ancestors were involved in any number of trades and skills. These included the buying and selling of wares, blacksmithing, tinsmithing, cap making, shopkeeping, and so on. Jews were also innkeepers. Jewish taverns were popular spots for Jews and Gentiles alike. Even when Jews were forbidden to own land, many were farmers, leasing the land and producing crops on it. Some Jews, while unable to own a farm, would still own cows and sell the milk products.

But it would be inaccurate to generalize about the history of Jewish business life in Eastern Europe. Since not all Jews lived in small towns, and since not all Jews lived in Eastern Europe (Many Jews lived in Western Europe, or the Middle East, or elsewhere), one could hardly think of an occupation which was not within the experience of some Jews somewhere.

I am always fascinated to learn about what my ancestors did for a living. I once heard a story about my grandmother's work which had a permanent influence on my vision of her. She was a dairy seller in Poland before she came to America.

A Jewish band of musicians from Galicia, home of my father's family for generations.

In 1923, my paternal grandfather came to the United States alone, leaving his pregnant wife and two children behind. He worked in the United States in order to save enough to send for them. Six years later he had saved enough to bring his wife and—now—three children to the United States, and he had a new apartment in Brooklyn, New York ready and waiting for his family.

But for six years my grandmother lived without her husband in a small town in southeast Poland, an area known as Galicia. She raised her three small children in a one-room apartment. She received a little money from her husband in America, but it wasn't much because he was trying to save enough to bring them to the United States. So my grandmother's dairy business was the real support for her young, growing family.

But she owned no cows. She traveled on foot from her town to buy milk from gentile farmers. Then she brought the milk back to town, churned some of it into butter, which she sold along with the milk.

Remember, she walked to the farms which were located outside the town, and the walk was not a short one—especially during the cold winter months. She carried two large milk pails which were heavy even when empty. When they were filled with milk, it was impossible for her to carry both pails at the same time. She picked up one of them, and walked with it as far as she could, and put it down. Then she turned around and walked back for the second, resting her arms along the way. Reaching the second pail, she picked it up and walked back to meet the first. Then she began the pattern once again.

My grandmother was not unique. Every family has stories about people like her. The process of collecting them from members of *your* family can be exciting and rewarding.

There are many reasons why the kinds of occupations we choose today are often different from the kinds our ancestors chose. But in some instances we find that our lives are very similar to theirs. My great great great grandfather, for example, was a writer. And I too am a writer. Even though two hundred years separate our lives, our career choices were similar. You may be surprised to learn how many different types of work are represented in your family history.

My Ancestors' Occupations

NAME OF ANCESTOR	RELATIONSHIP TO YOU	OCCUPATION	PLACE

HERE IS MY GRANDFATHER, YUDL KURZWEIL, LEANING ON HIS
metal-bending machine. He was trained as a tinsmith in Poland by his father.
They made pots and pans. When my grandfather came to America he used his
skills to become a roofer. He used this machine to make gutters for roofs. In
order for a gutter to catch the rain, it had to be curved.

MY MOTHER'S PARENTS WERE SHOPKEEPERS. THIS PHOTO,
taken about 50 years ago, shows them in front of their sewing machine shop.
Both my grandfather and my grandmother worked in the store. The woman on
the left was their employee.

Photographs of My Ancestors' Occupations

Try to locate photographs relating to the occupations of your ancestors and mount copies here.

NAME _____

RELATIONSHIP TO ME _____

OCCUPATION _____

LOCATION _____

NAME _____

RELATIONSHIP TO ME _____

OCCUPATION _____

LOCATION _____

Stories About My Ancestors' Occupations

Remember that a family story need not be long. The story about my grandmother's dairy business is only a few lines long. Record interesting or unusual stories relating to your ancestors' occupations.

_____

_____

_____

_____

_____

_____

_____

_____

_____

_____

_____

_____

_____

_____

_____

_____

_____

_____

_____

PARENTS' OCCUPATIONAL HISTORY

FATHER

MOTHER

JEWS OFTEN ORGANIZED INTO GROUPS BASED ON THEIR professions. In Eastern Europe, for example, many synagogues were established by occupational groups. There was the "tailor's shul" and the "carpenter's shul." It is no surprise that Jews became active in organizing unions in America. This is a group of "independent businessmen." The photograph was taken in Poland in the 1920's. My great grandfather, a tinsmith by trade, sits in the second row from the bottom, fifth from the left.

If you look at the current volume of the American Jewish Yearbook, you will find pages and pages of organizations listed. Some of the more well-known groups are B'nai B'rith, Hadassah, National Council of Jewish Women, ORT and the Jewish War Veterans. What Jewish organizations do you belong to? How about your parents, grandparents and great grandparents?

ORGANIZATIONS WE JOINED

NAME OF ORGANIZATION	FAMILY MEMBER(S) WHO BELONG(S)

CHAPTER 8
WHEN YOU GET MARRIED

When my grandmother died, my grandfather had to supply the U.S. Government with proof of their marriage.

All he had was a ketubah.

My grandmother had kept the ketubah, the Jewish marriage contract. Sixty-two years earlier, my grandfather had signed it in front of two witnesses. Sixty-two years earlier my grandfather and grandmother had stood under a huppah, a wedding canopy, and participated in an ancient Jewish rite making them husband and wife. My grandfather recited the same marriage formula that his father had said under a huppah, and that *his* father had said before him, and so on back through the generations.

I found their ketubah folded up in an envelope, in a small box where my grandfather had kept their most important papers. The ketubah was yellow with age; one of the folds was tearing a bit. But there it was, to photocopy and mail to the government, hopefully acceptable for official use.

Their ketubah was certainly all the proof my grandparents needed!

I looked carefully at the ketubah. It helped me to recreate an event which happened sixty-two years earlier. It told me facts like who, where, and when. But perhaps more importantly it got me ready for my own wedding day which took place just a few months later.

When I was preparing for my wedding, I knew that the details of the ceremony included certain set motions, words, and objects. And the sixty-two year old ketubah my grandparents used as part of *their* wedding reminded me that the patterns of my Jewish life share many details with Jews throughout the world today and with Jews throughout history.

When I signed a ketubah on the day of my wedding, I was repeating an action dating back to ancient times. The ketubah is a legal document. It has a very carefully worded text and must be filled in with accuracy. The details include who the bride and groom are, who the two witnesses are, where the wedding takes place, and who performs the wedding ceremony.

The signing of the ketubah often takes place before the marriage ceremony itself, but it is traditional for it to occur under the huppah. The huppah is a canopy which is held over the bride and groom during the wedding as a symbol of the new home they will create together.

When I stood under the huppah, looking at my bride, I recited the words, "Behold you are consecrated to me with this ring according to the laws of Moses and the people of Yisrael". These were the same words spoken by my father when he and my mother married, and there is little doubt that the very same words were spoken by my ancestors down through the ages at their weddings.

The ketubah of the author's grandparents—Samuel Gottlieb and Helen Klein   July 15, 1917   25 Tammuz 5678

THIS IS AN ENGLISH TRANSLATION OF PART OF MY KETUBAH.
Some day in the future, my descendants might find this ketubah and notice that the rabbi who performed my wedding had the same surname as my wife: Eidenbaum. With some investigation into our family history, my future descendants will discover that the rabbi was my wife's father, Rabbi Julius Eidenbaum of Newark, New Jersey.

THIS CERTIFICATE WITNESSETH THAT on the ....first.... ....day of the week, the ....first.... day of the month ....Teveth.... ...., in the year 574.2.. corresponding to the ..twenty-seventh day.. of ..December.. 1981., the holy Covenant of Marriage was entered into at ..East Meadow, New York.. between the Bridegroom ....Arthur Kurzweil.... and his Bride ....Rea Lee Eidenbaum.... ....

The said Bridegroom made the following declaration to his Bride:
"Be you my wife according to the law of Moses and Israel. I faithfully promise that I will be a true husband to you. I will honor and cherish you, protect and support you, and provide all that is necessary for your due sustenance, as it is becoming a Jewish husband to do. I also take upon myself all such further obligations for your maintenance, during your life-time, as are prescribed by our religious statute."

And the said Bride has pledged her faith to him, in affection and in sincerity, and has thus taken upon herself the fulfillment of all the duties incumbent upon a Jewish wife.

This Covenant of Marriage was duly executed and witnessed this day, according to the usage of Israel.

.... Bridegroom
.... Bride
.... Witness
.... Witness
.... Rabbi

My Parents' Ketubah

If you cannot locate your parents' ketubah to photocopy and paste here, see how much information you can discover about their wedding and record it on this page.

_____

and

_____

were united in marriage

in _____

on the _____ *day of* _____

in the year 19 _____ *corresponding to the* _____

day of _____ *in the year 57* _____

according to the laws of the State of

_____ *and in accordance*

with the customs of Israel

_____
RABBI

_____   _____
BRIDE   BRIDEGROOM

_____   _____
WITNESS   WITNESS

Jewish wedding ring from 18th century Italy symbolizes the importance of the home in Jewish family life.

WHEN A MAN GIVES A WOMAN AN OBJECT OF VALUE (IT NEED not be a ring) and recites the prescribed ancient formula in front of two qualified witnesses, then a legal Jewish marriage has taken place. There are many other customs used in traditional Jewish marriages, but they are not part of the minimum requirements. Individual families too have added special customs to their weddings. In some families the same wedding ring is used from generation to generation. In others, families use the same huppah at each wedding. In recent years, it has become popular for the bride and groom to recite personally prepared vows to express their own special feelings. Every Jewish wedding is unique in its own way. When you ask your parents and grandparents about their weddings, they will probably remember some custom or some incident to tell you about. Record their comments here.

My Grandparents' Ketubah

If you cannot locate your grandparents' ketubah to photocopy and paste here, see how much information you can discover about their wedding and record it on this page.

_____

and

_____

were united in marriage

in _____

on the _____ *day of* _____

in the year 19 _____ *corresponding to the* _____

day of _____ *in the year 57* _____

according to the laws of the State of

_____ *and in accordance*

with the customs of Israel

_____
RABBI

_____   _____
BRIDE   BRIDEGROOM

_____   _____
WITNESS   WITNESS

My Grandparents' Ketubah

If you cannot locate your grandparents' ketubah to photocopy and paste here, see how much information you can discover about their wedding and record it on this page.

_____

and

_____

were united in marriage

in _____

on the _____ *day of* _____

in the year 19 _____ *corresponding to the* _____

day of _____ *in the year 57* _____

according to the laws of the State of

_____ *and in accordance*

with the customs of Israel

_____
RABBI

_____   _____
BRIDE   BRIDEGROOM

_____   _____
WITNESS   WITNESS

IN THE 1920'S, MEMBERS OF THE KURZWEIL FAMILY GATHERED for a family wedding in the town of Jaraslaw, Poland. This photograph was taken. I received a copy from my cousin Joseph Schlaf, who lives in Warsaw, Poland. The young Mr. Schlaf is seated in the first row, center.

Family Weddings

_____AND_____
HUSBAND   WIFE

_____   _____
DATE   PLACE

_____   _____
CEREMONY CONDUCTED BY   TIME OF DAY

WITNESSES

ATTENDANTS

_____AND_____
HUSBAND   WIFE

DATE   PLACE

CEREMONY CONDUCTED BY   TIME OF DAY

WITNESSES

ATTENDANTS

_____AND_____
HUSBAND   WIFE

DATE   PLACE

CEREMONY CONDUCTED BY   TIME OF DAY

WITNESSES

ATTENDANTS

_____AND_____
HUSBAND   WIFE

DATE   PLACE

CEREMONY CONDUCTED BY   TIME OF DAY

WITNESSES

ATTENDANTS

_____AND_____
HUSBAND   WIFE

_____   _____
DATE   PLACE

_____   _____
CEREMONY CONDUCTED BY   TIME OF DAY

_____
WITNESSES

_____
ATTENDANTS

_____

_____AND_____
HUSBAND   WIFE

_____   _____
DATE   PLACE

_____   _____
CEREMONY CONDUCTED BY   TIME OF DAY

_____
WITNESSES

_____
ATTENDANTS

_____

_____AND_____
HUSBAND   WIFE

_____   _____
DATE   PLACE

_____   _____
CEREMONY CONDUCTED BY   TIME OF DAY

_____
WITNESSES

_____
ATTENDANTS

_____

_____AND_____
HUSBAND   WIFE

_____   _____
DATE   PLACE

_____   _____
CEREMONY CONDUCTED BY   TIME OF DAY

_____
WITNESSES

_____
ATTENDANTS

_____

BOTH OF THESE PHOTOGRAPHS ARE THE "OFFICIAL" WEDDING pictures of Avraham Abusch Kurzweil. But there are three important differences:

1) The grooms are different.
2) The brides are different
3) The centuries are different.

My great grandfather and I share the same Hebrew name. I was named after him. His wedding took place in 1890; mine occured in 1981.

His wife is Hinde Ruchel Lowenthal; my wife is Rea Lee Eidenbaum.

His wedding took place in Przemysl, Poland; mine was held in East Meadow, New York.

My Grandparents' Wedding Photographs

My Parents' Wedding Photograph

Family Wedding Photographs

CHAPTER 9
VISITING A JEWISH CEMETERY

Have you ever been to a Jewish cemetery? Unless a close relative or friend has died, you may never have gotten any closer to a cemetery than riding past one or walking past a cemetery's gates.

If you have never been inside a Jewish cemetery, you might think to yourself: While I'm curious to see what a cemetery is like, I'm lucky that I haven't needed to go to one yet. But a cemetery is not a place to avoid. Certainly we do not look forward to visiting a cemetery on the occasion of a death, but Jews go to cemeteries at other times as well. It is traditional, for example, to visit the graves of loved ones during the High Holiday season. It is also traditional to visit someone's grave on the anniversary of their death. Family historians, too, frequently visit cemeteries in order to gather historical information.

Every year, just before Rosh Hashanah, my father visits his parents' graves. He goes with his brother and sister—and I usually go with them. Each year, when I see my father, my uncle and my aunt standing before my grandparents' graves, I get the feeling that the family is together once again.

Cemeteries are monuments to memories. This is why we call a tombstone a "memorial stone." While we do not *need* a memorial stone to remember a deceased loved one, there is something special about visiting a grave, seeing a name engraved on the stone, and recalling the person that name represents.

Some people might think it sounds morbid, but I enjoy taking a walk through a Jewish cemetery. History comes alive in the cemetery as I walk past the graves and read the inscriptions. Sometimes, when I walk past a family plot, I can see over a hundred years of a family's history unfold. Remember that as Jews our Hebrew names are usually in the form of "_____, son/daughter of_____". In other words the names of the two generations appear on most memorial stones. Because of this, it is easy to wander through a family plot and construct a family tree.

On one of my trips to Eastern Europe I visited a tiny village in northeastern Hungary called Mateszalka. My mother's mother was born there. When I visited the shtetl I found that there were only two Jews still living in that town. A village which used to be bursting with Jewish life is no longer a Jewish town. Except for the two elderly Jews I met, it was as if no Jewish life had ever existed there.

The gates of the Jewish cemetery in Przemysl, Poland—the only remaining evidence of Jewish life in that city.

Until I went to the Jewish cemetery!

In the Jewish cemetery, as strange as this might sound, there was more evidence of Jewish *life* than anywhere else in this town that had once been a bustling shtetl. I felt a Jewish presence as I walked through the paths between the graves. I saw names and dates and constructed Jewish families. I knew that I stood where Jews for generations had also stood to bury their dead and to visit their graves.

And while there was no trace of anything Jewish in the entire town, the cemetery was filled with Hebrew letters. Each memorial stone seemed to say, "Read me. Read me."

I practiced my Hebrew with each grave I passed, reading names, dates, places, special inscriptions. I didn't understand it all, but I read each word anyway—for that is why they were there. To be read.

I walked up and down the rows, reading each of the stones. I suddenly found myself standing in front of the grave of my great-great grandmother! On her gravestone was her name and the name of her father. There I was, connected to six generations in my family. Over 150 years. All because I decided to visit a Jewish cemetery.

You can learn a lot in a Jewish cemetery. Most of all you get a sense that Jewish history is a long continuous chain—from generation to generation—from the ancient past to this very moment.

CHAIM YOSEF GOTTLIEB, MY GREAT GREAT GREAT GRAND-
father, was a Hasidic rabbi. Recently a cousin of mine, Herbert Tuchman,
traveled to Eastern Europe. When he located the rabbi's grave, he took this
photograph.

FAMILY CEMETERY RECORDS

When Jews set up a community, one of the first things they do is to establish a cemetery since there are specifically Jewish customs and regulations regarding death and burial. It is likely that your family has a cemetery plot—or even more than one for the different branches of your family. Try to find out the locations of your family's cemetery plots and the names of those buried there.

NAME _____ RELATIONSHIP _____

CEMETERY _____
            NAME   CITY

INSCRIPTION ON TOMBSTONE _____

_____

NAME _____ RELATIONSHIP _____

CEMETERY _____
            NAME   CITY

INSCRIPTION ON TOMBSTONE _____

_____

NAME _____ RELATIONSHIP _____

CEMETERY _____
            NAME   CITY

INSCRIPTION ON TOMBSTONE _____

_____

NAME _____ RELATIONSHIP _____

CEMETERY _____
           NAME   CITY

INSCRIPTION ON TOMBSTONE _____

_____

_____

NAME _____ RELATIONSHIP _____

CEMETERY _____
           NAME   CITY

INSCRIPTION ON TOMBSTONE _____

_____

_____

NAME _____ RELATIONSHIP _____

CEMETERY _____
           NAME   CITY

INSCRIPTION ON TOMBSTONE _____

_____

_____

NAME _____ RELATIONSHIP _____

CEMETERY _____
           NAME   CITY

INSCRIPTION ON TOMBSTONE _____

_____

_____

NAME _____ RELATIONSHIP _____

CEMETERY _____
           NAME   CITY

INSCRIPTION ON TOMBSTONE _____

_____

_____

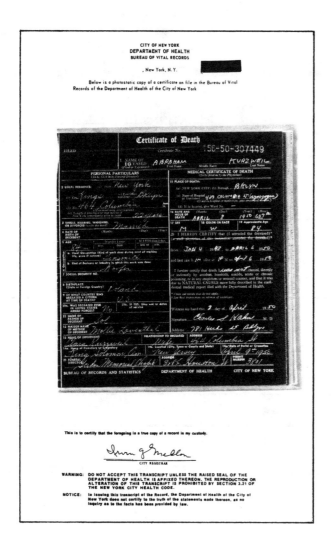

GOVERNMENT RECORD KEEPING HAS BEEN WITH US SINCE ancient times. One of the ways we can discover things about our families is to examine government records.

In the United States, and in many other countries as well, a Death Certificate must be filled out when a person dies. It is a requirement of law. I sent to the Health Department for my great grandfather's death certificate.

I already knew some things about him. First, since I was named after him, I knew his name. I also knew that he died in New York City. Since I was named after him, I knew that he must have died before the year 1951, the year I was born. (I am an Ashkenazi Jew, and the Ashkenazi custom, you will remember, is to name a child only after someone who has died.) The death certificate provided me with some additional information about my great grandfather. An item on the certificate indicates the place of death. I was surprised to learn that my great grandfather died in a synagogue.

When I discovered this fact and shared it with my father he then remembered that the place of his death had caused a problem. If a death occurs in a public place, the law requires that an autopsy be done to determine that the cause of death was natural. Autopsies are forbidden by Jewish law (with certain special exceptions). Since the synagogue is considered a public place, it took quite an effort to convince the Health Department to overlook the need for an autopsy.

I also saw on the certificate that my great grandfather's occupation was listed as "roofer". I already knew that he was a tinsmith, and now I discovered that my great grandfather used his tinsmith skills to build roofs too.

Family Yahrzeit Record

We traditionally remember the day of an individual's death rather than the day of birth. ''Birth and death are like two ships in a harbor. There is no reason to rejoice on the ship's setting out on a journey (birth), not knowing what may be encountered on the high seas, but we should rejoice at the ship's safe return to port (death).'' *(Levi, Exodus Rabbah, 48.1)*

The day of death is marked by lighting a memorial candle, a yahrzeit candle, and the recitation of the kaddish prayer.

NAME

RELATIONSHIP

HEBREW DATE OF DEATH

NAME

RELATIONSHIP

HEBREW DATE OF DEATH

NAME

RELATIONSHIP

HEBREW DATE OF DEATH

NAME

RELATIONSHIP

HEBREW DATE OF DEATH

NAME

RELATIONSHIP

HEBREW DATE OF DEATH

SIX MILLION JEWS WERE KILLED DURING THE HOLOCAUST. Those six million Jews constituted one third of all the Jews in the world. In other words, just a short time ago, one out of every three Jews in the world was murdered.

Since there are no graves or memorial stones for most of the victims of the Holocaust, I often see my family photograph album as a permanent memorial to those individuals in my family whose lives were taken.

Each person in these photographs was murdered during the Holocaust.

FAMILY PHOTOGRAPHS OF

HOLOCAUST VICTIMS

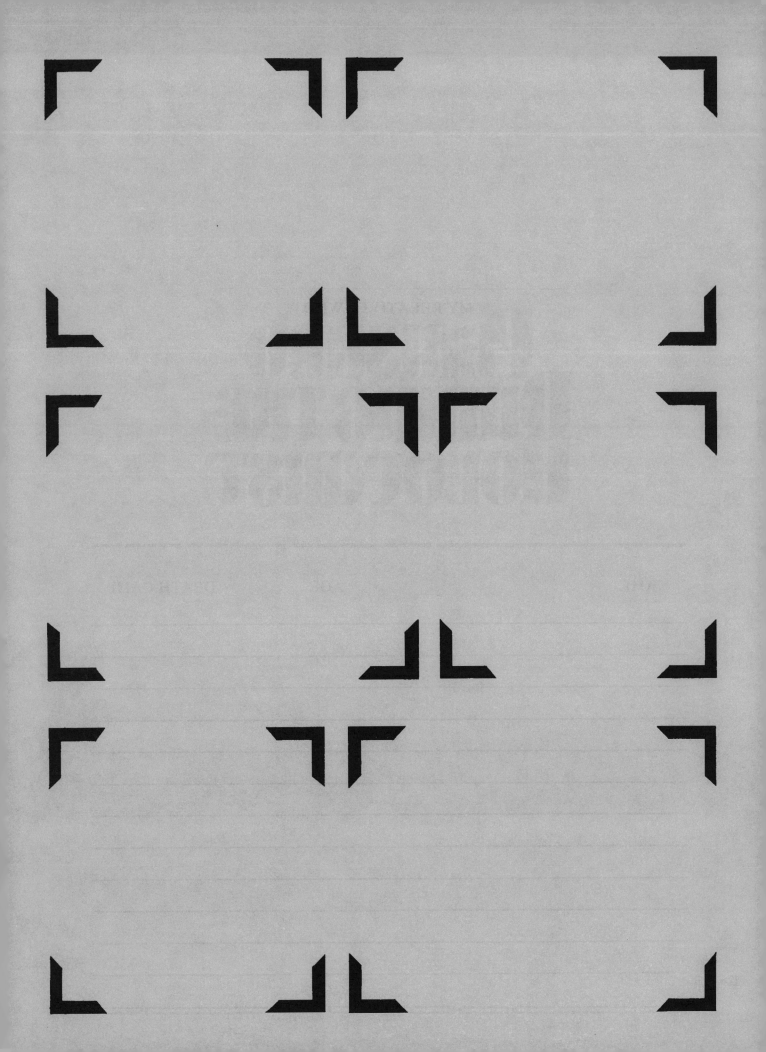

MY RELATIVES WHO
PERISHED DURING THE HOLOCAUST

NAME	AGE	DEATH CAMP

CHAPTER 10
CONCLUSION

Throughout our lives we constantly make decisions. We ask our friends to recommend records and movies. We ask people to suggest good restaurants. We generally rely on others for all kinds of information. And after we gather information, we make our own decisions.

In Judaism, we believe in the concept of Free Will. Ultimately, each of us decides what to do, what to think and what to be. We each decide for ourselves. We might decide to simply follow someone else's direction—but even then, the decision about whom to follow is still ours. Each of us is on our own. Whether we like it or not, we each have to make our own decisions.

In our lives as Jews, we make certain choices. We decide which holidays to observe, which rituals to practice, which prayers to say. Is there only one correct way to be Jewish? Some Jews say so, but many Jews disagree.

Who is an authentic Jew—a *real* Jew?

I will never forget how the famous Jewish writer Elie Wiesel answered that question. He said, "Each of us has to decide for himself. Can we say that an Israeli soldier, risking his life on the frontier to protect his people is not *authentic* because he doesn't put on tefillin? Of course not. He is an authentic Jew—he is an Israeli soldier, a significant member of the Jewish community and Jewish history."

Each of us is *already* an authentic Jew.

Each of us has the right to make our own choices about our Jewish lives, but we must remember that some choices have already been made for us. And the choices we make will affect those who come after us.

For instance, I live in the United States and my second cousin lives in Budapest, Hungary. Life in Budapest is very different from life in New York City. My grandmother decided to come to America seventy five years ago, while my cousin's grandmother chose to stay in Hungary. The two grandmothers made decisions that determined where their grandchildren would be born and what their lives would be like.

As I look back on my personal Jewish history, I see that it is made up of many people with different ways of doing things. My parents influenced my opinions, beliefs, and choices just as their parents contributed to theirs. As I examine my Jewish family history I obtain a better and better understanding of the people who made me the person I am and what my choices are.

You have had the opportunity in this book to gather a great deal of information about yourself and your family. I hope you will use it to help you make the important decisions in *your* life.

In the Talmud it is Recorded:

"The masters of Yavneh were in the habit of saying:
I am a creature and my fellow man is a creature. My work
is in the city and his work is in the field. I rise early to go
to my work, and he rises early to go to his work. As he
does not pride himself on his work, so I do not pride
myself on mine.
But should you think that I am doing more then he—we
have learned:
'Do more, do less, it matters not, so long as one's heart is
turned to heaven'''.

Ber. 17a